First Facts®

PREDATOR PROFILES

TIGERS

– BUILT FOR THE HUNT –

by Julia Vogel

Consultant: Dr. Jackie Gai, DVM
Wildlife Vet

raintree
a Capstone company — publishers for children

Raintree is an imprint of Capstone Global Library Limited, a company incorporated in England and Wales having its registered office at 7 Pilgrim Street, London, EC4V 6LB – Registered company number: 6695582

www.raintree.co.uk
myorders@raintree.co.uk

Editorial Credits
Brenda Haugen, editor; Juliette Peters, designer;
Tracy Cummins, media researcher; Katy LaVigne, production specialist

Printed in China.

ISBN 978 1 474 70195 2
19 18 17 16 15
10 9 8 7 6 5 4 3 2 1

British Library Cataloguing in Publication Data
A full catalogue record for this book is available from the British Library.

Photo Credits
FLPA: Gerard Lacz, 15; Getty Images: Andy Rouse, 9, Steve Winter, 13; Shutterstock: Anan Kaewkhammul, 2, Design Element, Anne-Marie B, Cover, Arangan Ananth, 7, Colette3, 5, Back Cover, Erika Kusuma Wardani, 16, Jean-Edouard Rozey, 3, Julian W, 19, Matthew Cole, 14, Michal Ninger, 4, Nachiketa Bajaj, 17, pashabo, Design Element, Sarah Cheriton-Jones, 12, Vaclav Volrab, 6, Volodymyr Burdiak, 10; Thinkstock: davemhuntphotography, 21, Fuse, 11, Martin Bornack, 18, ShinOkamoto, 1.

CONTENTS

BIG, STRONG CAT

A tiger quietly moves through the jungle. The hungry cat is searching for **prey**. Like other cats, tigers are **predators** that only eat meat. They hunt many types of prey such as deer and wild pigs.

The biggest tigers weigh 300 kilograms (660 pounds). They can kill a water buffalo that is twice their size.

FACT
Tigers live and hunt in the jungles, swamps and mountain forests of Asia.

prey animal hunted by another animal for food

predator animal that hunts other animals for food

4

NIGHT HUNTER

Tigers hunt at night. The cats' **keen** eyesight is six times better in darkness than a human's.

Sharp hearing also helps tigers at night. The snap of a twig gets a tiger's attention. Is it a wild pig, a deer or some other prey? The hunt is on!

FACT

Unlike other cats, tigers seem to like water. They swim to catch deer, crocodiles and other prey.

keen highly developed or extremely good

IMPORTANT SENSE

Tigers do not rely much on their sense of smell to find prey. But their sense of smell is still important. It helps tigers to know where to hunt. Each tiger leaves droppings, and rubs against trees, to mark its hunting **territory**. These **scent marks** warn other tigers to stay away.

FACT

The size of a tiger's territory depends on how many prey animals live there. Jungles rich in wildlife can feed more tigers.

territory area of land that an animal claims as its own to live in

scent mark smell to warn other animals to stay away

HIDDEN HUNTER

A tiger can run fast, but not very far. Some prey animals, such as antelopes, can outrun a tiger over a long distance. Instead of chasing prey, a tiger **stalks** its prey. Its padded paws help it to move in silence.

FACT

Tigers can **sprint** 56 kilometres (35 miles) per hour.

stalk hunt an animal in a hidden, quiet way

sprint run fast over a short distance

A tiger hides and waits to catch prey by surprise. In thick grasses, a tiger's orange and black fur provides **camouflage**. Prey cannot spot its hidden enemy. The prey steps closer. The hungry tiger waits. At last, the prey moves within reach.

FACT

Each tiger has its own pattern of stripes. The pattern is as unique as a human fingerprint. No two people have the same fingerprints.

camouflage pattern or colour on an animal's skin or fur that makes it blend in with the things around it

The tiger leaps! Its huge body slams down on the prey. The tiger's sharp claws hold on tight. Its long **canine** teeth bite deep into the prey's neck. The tiger's powerful jaws crush the animal's bones.

A tiger can eat 30 kilograms (66 pounds) of meat in one meal. A tiger may feed on a big kill for four days, and not eat again for two weeks.

FACT
To keep their claws sharp, tigers tuck them inside their paws when not in use.

canine long, pointed tooth

LEARNING TO HUNT

Like other **mammals**, female tigers make milk for their young. The 1.4-kilogram (3-pound) newborn tigers drink milk for up to three months. After that the mother starts to bring them meat. When the cubs are six months old, they follow their mother on their first hunt.

At first, cubs watch their mother. She teaches them how to stalk, wait and kill.

FACT
Male tigers do not help to bring up the cubs.

mammal warm-blooded animal that breathes air; mammals have hair or fur; female mammals feed milk to their young

Cubs also learn to hunt by playing together. Playing builds muscles for running and pouncing. Later, they practise killing small animals such as **piglets** and **fawns**. Cubs stay with their mothers until they can catch enough food to survive.

piglet young pig

fawn young deer

YOUNG PREDATORS

By the time they are two years old, the cubs are fully grown. Young adult females find territories close to their mothers. Young adult males often wander far away. Each tiger is ready to hunt on its own.

FACT

Although adult tigers live alone, they sometimes share a kill with other tigers that live near by.

AMAZING BUT TRUE!

Tigers have the largest canine teeth of all big cats. These teeth can be as long as an adult human finger! A tiger's canines are strong, too. They won't break even when a tiger bites through thick bone.

GLOSSARY

camouflage pattern or colour on an animal's skin or fur that makes it blend in with the things around it

canine long, pointed tooth

fawn young deer

keen highly developed or extremely good

mammal warm-blooded animal that breathes air; mammals have hair or fur; female mammals feed milk to their young

piglet young pig

predator animal that hunts other animals for food

prey animal hunted by another animal for food

scent mark smell to warn other animals to stay away

sprint run fast over a short distance

stalk hunt an animal in a hidden, quiet way

territory area of land that an animal claims as its own to live in

READ MORE

All About Tigers (Text Structures: Description Text), Philip Simpson (Raintree, 2014)

Animals in Danger in Asia, Richard and Louise Spilsbury (Raintree, 2013)

Tigers (Usborne Beginners), James Maclaine (Usborne Publishing Ltd, 2012)

WEBSITES

www.bbc.co.uk/nature/life/Tiger

Learn more about tigers.

http://gowild.wwf.org.uk/asia

Learn more about tigers in Asia.

www.ngkids.co.uk/did-you-know/10-tiger-facts

Ten fascinating facts about tigers!

COMPREHENSION QUESTIONS

1. How do tiger cubs learn to hunt?

2. What is a territory? Look at the photo on page 9. What do you think this tiger is doing?

INDEX